CELL WARS II

VIRUS INVASION

A. MILES

ILLUSTRATED BY N.P.MONAGHAN

ISBN: 150318661X
ISBN 13: 9781503186613
A CIP catalogue record for this book is available from the British Library.

AM – For Paul x

And Nerys, Marissa, William, Lewis, Bailey, Sammy, Oli, Josh, Maddie, Joe, Patrick and Grace x

NPM – For Robert and Rhys x

MAP OF VEINS AND ARTERIES

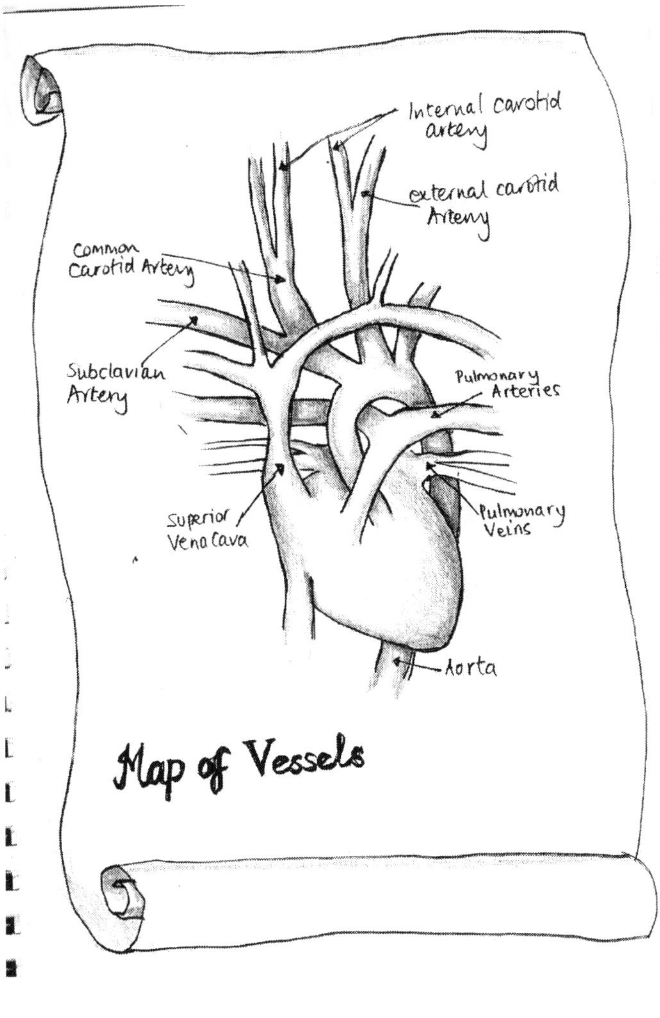

INTRODUCING

Phyllis

Haemo (*Hemo*) and Globin

PROLOGUE

Have you ever been ill? Most people get ill at some time in their lives. Hopefully, it was just a cold, or something that disappeared after you took some medicine.

Being ill is not very nice. Your head might hurt, or maybe you feel sick. Some illnesses are over very quickly, but some can last a long time.

Bacteria and viruses make us ill. Some bacteria can cause horrible illnesses, like pneumonia or meningitis.

Food poisoning is when you have eaten something with the bacteria in. It normally makes you sick and you need to go the toilet a lot! It's your body's way of trying to get rid of the bacteria.

The white blood cells inside your body try to kill the bacteria, but sometimes they need help. Doctors can help with a special medicine called antibiotics. Do you remember in the last story of 'Cell Wars' that the bacteria made more of itself by splitting in half? Bacteria are living things. They are alive. Antibiotics can attack bacteria and kill them, so you feel better again.

Viruses are different. Viruses are not alive like bacteria. They are machines like computers (think of the words 'computer virus'). Viruses make more of themselves by invading another cell's body, just like a hermit crab tries to get inside another crab's shell.

Do you know the name of a virus? No? I'm sure you do, but you may not have realised. A 'cold' is a virus. Yes, remember that time you were sneezing and feeling horrible and your mum said it was a cold. She was right. It was a cold, but a virus caused it.

Viruses are very clever. They have been around for a long time too. Have you heard of the flu? Yes? Well, that's a virus. Its proper name is influenza. What about chicken pox? Measles? Ebola? They are all viruses.

Sometimes they are very serious. So serious that when you were a small baby, the person who looked after you would have taken you to the doctors, so you could be immunised. You won't remember it, but the doctor or nurse gave you an injection. In that injection was the actual virus. I'm not joking! They gave you a tiny amount of the virus so that the white blood cells in your body could fight against this new enemy, and remember it. If you ever got the virus again, your body would know how to attack it. Clever!

Your body is amazing. It has lots of ways to stop the harmful germs or 'microbes' getting in. Do you know why you cough? Because you have something stuck in your throat? Well, in some ways this is true. When you have a cold, a tiny microbe, 'the virus', irritates your throat whilst trying to get further inside. Your body's special army (nerve endings send signals to the brain) warns your body what is happening, and your body reacts by coughing to get rid of it.

The same happens when we sneeze. Inside our noses are hairs that behave like guards or soldiers. Tiny, broom-like guards trap invaders and things that irritate our noses. The special army sends the warning signal and then you sneeze at speeds up to 100mph. That's fast!

And it happens so quickly we can't get a tissue in time and we sneeze into the air around us. The problem is that those little microbes, that are trying to get into your body, will also try and get into someone else's and make them ill. I told you viruses are clever! (Tip - try sneezing into your jumper or top, instead of your hands).

Imagine a virus has managed to get inside you. Maybe you didn't wash your hands properly (using soap!) after you had sneezed on them and then you ate a sandwich. That virus is now making its way through your body. It's going to try and make you ill. The doctor can't give you antibiotics this time. They don't work on viruses. The antibiotics don't recognise the viruses now because they are disguised.

So, how do we kill them? When the

viruses are very dangerous, like ebola, scientists develop special medicines to help. But when we get viruses like flu, then rest, healthy food and lots of water is the best thing to help in the fight inside you. Why? Your special army of white blood cells are going to find and attack the virus for you.

Remember Bands, the white blood cell character from Cell Wars? He's still inside you, helping to fight against your enemies and trying to stay out of trouble.

Now, use your imagination and let's go deeper into your body. Go under the skin near the top of your arm and into a blood vessel. It's an artery. The subclavian artery. Up ahead you can see another tunnel crossing into this one. The Aorta. Let's watch and see what happens this time.

CHAPTER

1

Bands was alone and on an operation. A very important operation. He scanned the area from his lookout position, nestled safely in the cell wall, at a crossway between the Aorta and subclavian artery.

"Open!" he commanded. The nucleus panel, across his middle, opened up to reveal the computer screen.

Information was flashing up, but first, Bands needed to identify the invader.

He took out his cellescopic binoculars. Slowly they came into focus and Bands began to track the moving blood cells in the artery. With his binoculars pressed firmly to his head, he zoomed in on a small group of red blood cells. Pressing the photo button, he took an image of the cells, which was then sent to his computer screen.

Almost immediately, information about the cells flashed up on the screen.

HEALTH: 80%
AGE: 4 DAYS
LOCATION: PULMONARY ARTERY
DESTINATION: FEMORAL ARTERY
IDENTIFICATION: RED BLOOD CELL
ACTIVITY: RETURNING TO LUNGS TO PICK UP OXYGEN

'*Okay*!' Bands thought to himself. '*No danger here*'. The binoculars continued to capture images of all the moving cells and each time, information was fed back to Bands' computer. Bands watched the screen change. Suddenly, something caught Bands' eye.

"What's that?" said Bands. A different image flashed up on the screen. This wasn't a red blood cell. It was purple in colour and round like a slightly pointed cocci bacterium. He had met that enemy on his last mission. The computer churned out the information it had on this intruder.

HEALTH: 100%

AGE: 1 HOUR OLD

LOCATION: PULMONARY ARTERY

DESTINATION: LUNGS

IDENTIFICATION: BACTERIUM CALLED PNEUMONIA

ACTIVITY: TO INFILTRATE LUNGS

Bands knew this bacterium was dangerous. If it got into the lungs it would start to multiply and the lungs would become inflamed. Then the lungs wouldn't be able to get oxygen into the red blood cells, and take the carbon dioxide away. Using his cell phone, he dialed the emergency code.

"This is a code red, I repeat a code red." Bands' voice echoed over the cell sound system, alerting the rest of his team patiently waiting for the call to action.

Closing his nucleus panel, Bands swam out into the stream of red blood cells.

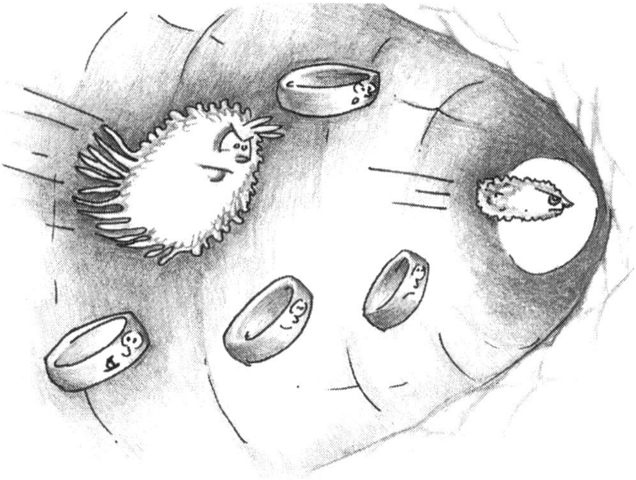

Bumping and colliding into the red blood cell surfers, he tried desperately to catch up with the purple invader. The speed was much slower here in the vein and he had to go through the valve doors too. Bands forced his way past some of the slower, deflated red blood cells up to the next valve door.

“Do you still see the invader?” said a voice on Band’s cell phone. It was Captain

Neutro keeping an eye on him.

"Yes, Sir! It is trying to hide in the pack of red blood cells, but I can still see a glimpse of it. I won't let it out of my sight."

"Good luck soldier!" said Captain Neutro, and then the line went dead.

Bands was on his own once more. He continued to chase the enemy deeper down the vein tunnel. He knew he had to stick to the operation and what was required from him. He could do this. At a sharp corner the red blood cells slowed down, leaving the purple bacterium exposed. This was his chance. He increased his speed and came up behind the enemy.

"Amo," he shouted. The nucleus panel opened and out came the suction gun. By now, the purple invader knew Bands was after him and tried to accelerate away. Bands gave chase, his body stretching out, ready to swallow.

Down came the cellophane visor screen and Bands locked into the enemy's movement. The beeps signaled he was in range and locked in. Bands fired out the poison from the toxic gun to paralyse the invader, and then in one swift gulp sucked him up with the suction gun. He'd done it, but he couldn't stop yet. The fight was only just beginning.

Up ahead he could see more purple bodies. Bands knew they had now multiplied and it was only going to get worse.

He charged ahead bumping into the pink padded walls of the vein. This bumping action propelled him faster down the tunnel. Bands could feel the adrenaline pumping around him. He locked in to another invader and shot him with his poison. There were lots more of the purple invaders now.

They continued to multiply. Bands became quite frenzied in the heat of the action. He shot one, then another, shooting and sucking the enemies in. The red blood cells stopped swimming so they could watch Bands and point out where the invaders were.

"Bands! Over here!" shouted out one red blood cell.

"Watch out, Bands!" shouted another.

"Behind you!" shouted a third.

Bands just kept shooting. There were so many now and it was becoming chaotic.

"Be careful, Bands," said a friendly voice behind him. It was Phyllis, the giggly white blood cell from his class. His backup team had finally arrived.

"Am I glad to see you!" said Bands, who didn't feel quite complete without his team. "Right guys, spread out!" he ordered.

As they continued down the tunnel,

Bands quickly updated the team on what they were dealing with. “This purple invader is called pneumonia. It causes swelling in our human’s airways, making it hard to breathe and our human could die. We need to stop them at the heart, before they can go into the pulmonary artery which goes into the lungs.”

Bands and his team were now within range of a large clump of purple invaders. Bands gave the order and the white blood cells (WBCs) charged. They locked in and began shooting. The cells were beginning to bump into each other in this small area, and it was getting hot.

Bands looked up from his position to see what was happening, as he had been trained to do. The white blood cells, with all the excitement and adrenaline pumping around, were becoming chaotic and trigger-happy. They were shooting at anything now. Soon they would begin to shoot each other.

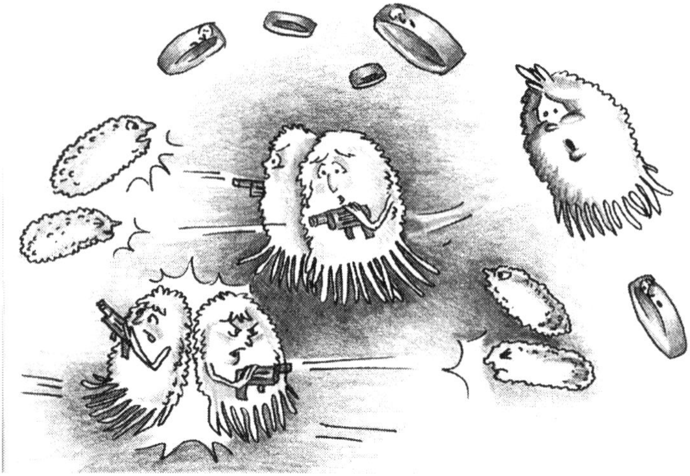

Shots of poison went over Bands' head just missing him.

"Stop!" commanded Bands, but his team couldn't hear him in all the confusion and noise.

"Oh no! This is a disaster," said Bands. "Stop!" he shouted again. Just as he did so, he turned and saw Phyllis. He watched the poison flying right at her. He swam as quickly as he could, but it was too late.

"What have you done?" Bands shouted at the white blood cell that had shot Phyllis.

Just then, bells went off in the tunnel. Lights flashed on and off and a voice boomed out. "Simulation ended, Simulation ended! Enemy alive and multiplying in the lungs. Mission failed."

A deflated Bands, slumped down onto the tunnel floor. Captain Neutro, appeared at his side.

"Is Phyllis okay?" Bands asked.

"She's fine," replied Captain Neutro. "We didn't use real poison. This was a practice mission remember. Unfortunately, you didn't complete it successfully so it's back to school for you."

Bands had failed. Again! Was he ever going to be a Cell Captain?

CHAPTER

2

Bands stared through the window of the Bone Marrow school, where blood cells are made. Lightning bolts crackled overhead. Over by the great Hall of the Vena Cava, Bands could see rows and rows of red spherical discs; the red blood cells. They were all silent, bobbing up and down on the spot. This was strange. The red blood cells were never silent! They loved to charge around riding the waves and basically having a good time. '*It must be great to be a red blood cell,*' Bands thought to himself. '*Nothing seemed to bother them.*'

"Good afternoon, Bands!" said Master Baso, gliding up behind him. "I see you are watching the red blood cells passing out parade."

Bands turned around to face Master Baso. "Their passing out parade? Already? But they've only just arrived."

"Now, now, Bands. We each have a job to do and theirs is different to ours."

"Yes, but I'm still training and I've been here for longer. It's not fair!" Bands started to play with his legs, wrapping the white spindly hairs around each other.

"Have you forgotten your position?" said Master Baso, staring at Bands. "You are part of the white cell army. Your job is very special and not every cell can do it."

Master Baso's eyes went all goggly when he was annoyed. Bands tried to sit up and unravel his legs, which were now in a knot. "Sorry, Sir! It's just I thought after the last battle my training would be over and I could go on missions by myself."

"Well, that is part of the reason why I asked you to come here today. You have worked hard with your training and are studying the blood paths more now, but I heard about your practice mission this morning. I understand it did not go well?"

Bands nodded. "I know how frustrating it can be, so I would like you to be my classroom assistant. You know what it's like to be young and enthusiastic. You can help the new white blood cells channel all that energy and hopefully stay out of trouble."

"I'd be honoured, Sir!" said a delighted Bands, who had already begun to think of all the drills he could lead the new WBCs in.

"And one day soon, it will be your passing out parade," reassured Master Baso, his kindly eyes twinkling.

The sound of cheering made Bands look out of the window. It was the red blood cells, no longer silent, and bumping into each other.

"Why is their training only seven days?" Bands asked.

Master Baso glided away from the window towards his desk at the front of the classroom. "Their training is short because their lives are short. As you know, red blood cells carry the oxygen our humans need to all of its organs and take the carbon dioxide away. But they can only do this for about four months. Their bodies become exhausted from this strenuous job. New red blood cells are made to renew the dying ones."

Bands sat down in front of Master Baso's desk. "I had no idea. So, the guys I was talking to last month are probably dead by now?"

Master Baso nodded. Bands was quiet, his mind whirring. "How long do we live for then?"

"That's a difficult question to answer. We are more complex and therefore our life expectancy is more complex too."

"I get that," said Bands, "but you must have a rough idea?"

Master Baso looked at Bands and sighed. He opened up his nucleus. "Database open," commanded Master Baso. A string of letters and numbers filled up the screen and the interactive whiteboard in the classroom. The figures converted into pie charts, tables and venn diagrams, each showing life expectancy of a white blood cell.

"As you can see, a white blood cell can live anywhere between three years and six months," said Master Baso.

"Six months!" exclaimed Bands. "Is that all?"

"It depends on many factors," continued Master Baso, "including how many times in their life they have killed bacteria and what type of white blood cell they are."

Bands stared at the charts, his mouth wide open. Why had he never seen this before? Why had he never thought of this before?

"A cell can die in many ways. Overheating, a lack of oxygen, even poisoning and, of course, many of us die in battle trying to defeat the bacteria and viruses. Some even program themselves to self-destruct."

Bands looked up at Master Baso. "Some actually kill themselves! Why would they do that?"

Master Baso stopped using his teacher voice and looked at Bands. "Life cannot continue indefinitely. It has to end one day. It's nature's way of weeding out old and ineffective cells."

"How old are you, Sir?" Bands asked

the question before he had thought about how he would react to the answer.

"I'm getting old, Bands. I've been around for nearly three years now."

'*Nearly three years! The maximum time,*' Bands thought to himself.

Master Baso smiled at Bands. He knew what he had been thinking. "Don't worry young Bands. I'm not going anywhere just yet."

Just then, the school bell rang bringing their conversation to an end.

"Close information!" ordered Master Baso, and the diagram on the interactive board disappeared. Young, white blood cells all filed into the room and took up their positions in the spongy, pink padding of the tissue classroom. Suddenly the room lit up because of the lightning bolts outside, and Bands looked at Master Baso more closely then he had ever done before. Then the lights went out and his teacher's face vanished.

CHAPTER

3

The next day, Phyllis glided into the classroom. She smiled as she went past Bands.

"Thanks for trying to save me

yesterday," she said.

"Shame I didn't!" replied Bands.

"Don't be too hard on yourself. It was a difficult mission."

Bands knew she was trying to be nice, but he didn't need reminding that he had failed. He sat down next to her in a row of cells, like children sitting together on a squashy sofa.

Master Baso was waiting for silence before he began. "Today," he boomed, "we will be looking at the red blood cells and their job in the human body. Okay, open up your eye pads."

Each of the young cells flipped open one of their eyes and took out their portable tablets. "Please scan to page thirty four. Here you will see a detailed picture of a red blood cell." Master Baso continued. "Note how the red blood cell's body is perfectly spherical, with a slightly concave shape which forms its middle. Why do you think their shape is different to ours?"

Phyllis put up her hand. "It's because they don't have a nucleus, a middle bit. Their shape is flexible and they can squeeze into small spaces."

"Good," replied Master Baso. "And why is that important?"

"They take oxygen around the body and can squeeze into the tiny capillaries to get the oxygen to the muscles and organs."

"Good, good!" Master Baso nodded in approval. Bands stared at Phyllis. She was a quick learner and always had her hand up. Not like him.

"Phyllis is correct," continued Master Baso. "This is the main job of the red blood cells."

"Do they have a specific route or pathway?" asked one of the newer blood cells, who had been made that morning in the Bone Marrow.

"Could you all look at the screen now?" said Master Baso. All the cells looked up at the large projection screen, on the padded tissue floor wall next to Master Baso. "Bands, would you mind coming here, please? I'd like you to explain."

"Good luck!" whispered Phyllis, as

Bands moved to the front of the classroom.

He began. “The red blood cells pick up the oxygen from the lungs here and put it in their oxygen tanks. They then move into the heart. From the heart they travel through the arteries, taking the oxygen around the body.” Bands pointed it out on the screen. “When they have no more oxygen left, they pick up the carbon dioxide produced by the body, and take it back to the heart. Then they go through the pulmonary artery to the lungs. Here they get rid of the carbon dioxide and refill their oxygen tanks, ready to restart the journey.”

"An excellent explanation, Bands. I couldn't have said it better myself. You would make a great teacher, if you decided that there is more to life than going on missions."

Bands frowned and floated back to his seat. Master Baso continued to talk. "The major organs in the body are all connected by this amazing network system of paths. Although the red blood cells job is routine, there are times when they are called to action above their daily duties. Does anyone know when that is?"

Phyllis's hand shot up again. "When a human exercises, they need extra oxygen at the site of the muscles."

"Excellent work again. I see you have been doing your homework," enthused Master Baso, glancing over at Bands to see if he was listening.

He wasn't. Bands was staring out of the window watching the red blood cells. They were talking and messing around, as their Captain was trying to make himself heard over all the noise. It looked to Bands like they were receiving orders. '*Probably going on an exciting mission somewhere*,' Bands thought to himself.

"Now class, turn to page sixty five and see if you can answer the questions with your partner," said Master Baso. "Bands! Come here, please!" Bands looked up and glided towards his teacher, ready to be told off for daydreaming.

"I'd like you to go out with the red blood cells this afternoon. I have authorised it with their Captain, and he will allow you to accompany them on their mission to pick up oxygen. Two red blood cells will help show you the way."

"And keep me out of trouble!" said Bands laughing.

"Hmm! Something like that. Return here at 03.00 hours. Dismissed!"

"Thank you, Sir," replied Bands, as he sailed out of the classroom and into a mission.

CHAPTER

4

"Right, lads! I know you're excited but we have work to do," commanded the Red Blood Cell (RBC) Captain. "Pick up your tanks and let's try and get into some kind of order."

Bands floated up to the Captain. "Reporting for duty, Sir!"

The RBC Captain turned to face Bands. "At ease, soldier. We're not as disciplined as you white blood cells."

Bands looked around. The red cells were still laughing and joking and they didn't seem to be bothered about listening to their captain. '*Captain Neutro would never stand for this*,' Bands thought to himself.

Just then two red blood cells approached. "Hi. I'm Haemo and this is Globin," said the larger of the two blood cells. "Captain told us to show you around and answer any questions you may have. If we can, eh, Globin." The two blood cells began to laugh.

"Thanks. That would be great," said

Bands, not sure if these two were serious or not. “I’m still training to be a WBC, so don’t get to go on many missions at the moment.”

The two red blood cells looked at each other and then looked at Bands. “What! You mean you asked to come on this mission?” said Haemo.

Bands nodded.

“Wow! That’s seriously addicted, man! We don’t want to go on these missions. We just like to have fun. Don’t we Globin?”

Globin turned to face him. “Sorry, Haemo. What did you say? Wasn’t listening.

What are we doing again?"

Haemo began to laugh. "You're so laid back, man! Anymore laid back and you'd be lying down."

"I'd love a lie down," said Globin yawning. "Was up late last night 'cell-e-brating'. It's a new dance craze!" Haemo and Globin both started laughing. Bands didn't understand what they were talking about.

"Well, we've gotta go. You ready, Bands?" Haemo asked.

"Yes, Sir," Bands replied.

"Oh, just call me Haemo and don't bother calling Globin anything. He'll probably be asleep!" He laughed out loud again and this time Bands joined in. Their laughing was infectious.

The two red blood cells picked up their oxygen tanks and attached them to the underneath of their bodies. The other red blood cells had already gone on ahead. Bands began to swim after them.

“Hey, slow down,” called out Globin. “What’s the rush?”

“Your team has already gone. I thought we should catch them up,” said Bands.

“We don’t need to rush around,” said Haemo, joining them. “Just a routine job. We all get there eventually. And don’t forget there’s a lot more of us, than you white blood cells. We don’t wanna get stuck now, do we?”

“Where are we going?” asked Bands, who wasn’t sure if his companions even knew.

“The Holy Grail, man!” said Globin.

“The mother ship!” said Haemo.

Bands looked at them confused. He had no idea what they were talking about. Haemo and Globin laughed at Band’s puzzled face.

"The lungs, man. It's where it all begins." Haemo and Globin swam down the vein tunnel, followed by a nervous Bands.

The veins were harder to swim in. You had to push against the large vein doors for them to open up and allow you into the next part of the tunnel.

Bands watched Haemo and Globin swimming ahead, taking it in turns to push each other out of the way, especially when they approached the vein doors. One of them would always end up smashing into it, while the other would laugh hysterically until it was their turn.

'*This would never happen with the WBCs*' thought Bands, but he kept that to himself.

The tunnels flowed into each other until finally they started to widen and Bands, Haemo and Globin were propelled into a much larger area, crowded with red blood cells. There was a strong metallic smell in the air.

Haemo looked at Bands puzzled face. "It's iron! The smell. We carry it in our bodies." Haemo moved further into the room, as Bands followed. "This is the waiting room. The tissue wall is next to the lungs. We all come here to fill up on oxygen and then move on. It's why it's so crowded. It gets a bit mental in here."

Bands couldn't believe that it could get anymore crazy with this lot. Just then an alarm bell rang. "What's that?" said Bands.

"Time to fill up!" shouted Haemo and Globin, at the same time.

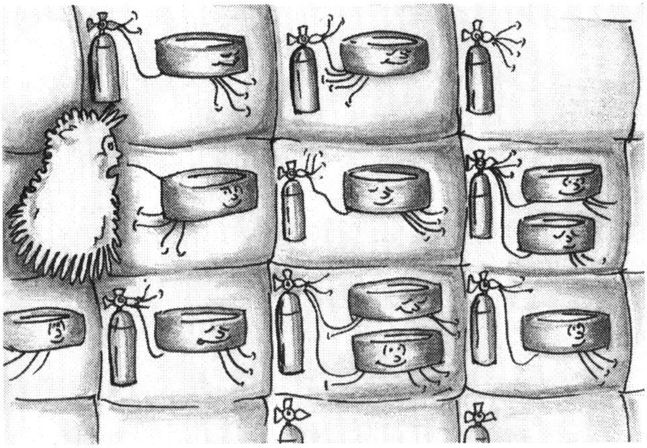

Bands watched as the red blood cells unplugged their tanks from underneath their bodies, and attached it to the tiny hair like fibres jutting out from the lung tissue walls. A whistle signaled when they were full of oxygen, and the red blood cells pushed the tanks back under their bodies once more.

“Ready, Bands? Let’s go surfing!” shouted Globin.

The doors of the waiting room opened and all the red blood cells rushed out into the pulmonary vein tunnel, causing a tidal wave behind them.

Bands bobbed up and down in the repeating wave, just managing to keep up with Haemo and Globin, which was important as the RBCs all looked the same to Bands!

They made their way into the heart.

Bands asked, “Where are we going?”

“You ask a lot of questions?” replied Haemo.

“ I know,” said Bands. “Sorry!”

“Chill, man! It’s cool! We normally don’t get asked anything. Everyone thinks we’re dumb.”

“Just because we don’t have a nucleus thingy. It isn’t fair,” said Globin. “What I could do if I had one of those computer thingymajigs! It would be awesome, man!”

“Yeah, until you had to do some work,” replied Haemo laughing.

“Work? Yeh, forgot about that. Maybe I wouldn’t like one after all!” He and Haemo began laughing like a couple of hyenas.

They eventually stopped, remembering Bands was still there. “What did you ask again?”

“Where are you going?’ repeated Bands.

“Oh, yeh! I remember,” said Globin. “Well, to be truthful, we don’t know. We just all speed out and listen to the contractions of the muscles.”

Haemo continued. “When the human is exercising, their muscles contract, you know, squeeze together. This signals for the heart to beat faster. And when the heart beats faster, we hear the call and move in the tunnels to get the oxygen to the muscles.”

“Cool!” said Bands, impressed for the first time that these two actually knew what they were doing.

The next tunnel was the Aorta, and they were propelled along at great speed. The red blood cells were good swimmers. They needed to be because of the strong currents in the arteries. The tunnels began to get smaller.

Haemo and Globin swam down the tiny capillaries that linked to the muscles.

"I'll stay here," Bands shouted after them. He knew he might get stuck down there because of his nucleus. Haemo and Globin could change their shape so they would be okay. Seconds later, Haemo and Globin were out and continued to the next capillary tunnel.

Haemo glanced at the dial on his oxygen tank. "I'm nearly out of gas," he said. "I'll have to head back to the lungs waiting room and fill up again."

"Sure thing. See you later," said Globin. "Bands, you can stay with me if you like?"

"Cool!" said Bands, warming to these strange blood cells.

Just then a signal boomed out, a signal Bands recognized. "Hold that thought, Globin. I've got to go. We have a code Red emergency."

"Well, you gotta go, when you gotta go! Good to meet you, Bands."

The two blood cells shot off in opposite directions; both protecting the body, but in different ways.

CHAPTER

5

Bands made his way to the top of the Aorta artery. The code Red signal requested all WBCs to assemble at this meeting point.

'We must have a mission near the human's head,' Bands thought to himself. The other WBCs soon joined Bands. They slowed down when they saw Captain Neutro, Captain Mono and Commander Lympho himself, standing in front of the tissue wall with a very serious look on their faces.

Within seconds, the noise of everyone arriving had subsided, and the WBCs were staring intently at their Commander waiting for instructions.

A large artery map was projected on the tissue wall behind them. Captain Mono spoke first. “Cells, open up your screens now.” Bands commanded his nucleus to open and looked down at his computer screen.

“On your screens you will see a digital image of a virus called ‘flu’ or ‘influenza’. We have had warnings that this virus has been spotted travelling through the Carotid artery.”

Bands stared at the picture in front of him. A round purple ball covered with yellow spiky sticks. It didn't look very friendly.

"This invader is extremely dangerous," continued Captain Neutro. "Viruses, like this one, are not cells. They cannot make more of themselves by splitting in two and then four, like bacteria. But don't be fooled. They are extremely clever."

" Sir! What do they want?' asked Bands.

"They want to make more of themselves. More viruses means a more powerful army and then they can kill all of us good cells and eventually our human body," explained Captain Mono.

"How can they do that?" asked Bands.

"They find a way in," joined in Commander Lympho. "They look for a weak spot in our cell structure and get past the tissue cells guarding the area. Once in, they try to get inside the bodies of other cells like us WBCs. They manage to disguise themselves and they continue to make more viruses."

Bands had never been involved in a situation like this before.

"Somehow they are getting past the guard cells, near the base of the throat, and moving along the Carotid artery," said Captain Mono. "We need a team to investigate where this virus is entering the body, and how they are doing it?"

"Another team will be deployed to the

top of the Aorta branch to stop the enemies who have already got in," finished off Captain Neutro.

Captain Mono began to call out the names of the first team. Bands and Phyllis heard their names. "Yes, Sir!" they responded and put away their computer screens. When the rest of the WBCs had been given their orders, they left, leaving Bands, Phyllis and a small group of WBCs headed up by Captain Neutro.

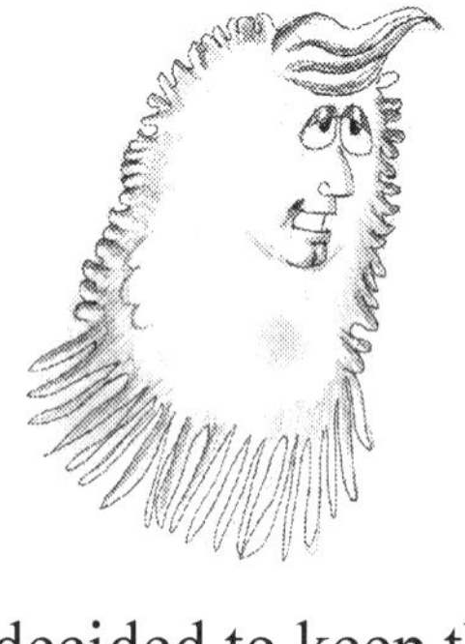

"We've decided to keep this team quite small," explained Captain Neutro, "as we don't want you to be noticed. Your job is to acquire information, not to kill the enemy. This is a delicate operation and needs trustworthy WBCs who can assess the situation and report back, not get involved. I know you are the right team to do that."

Bands felt extremely proud. At last he had an opportunity to show everyone that he could be trusted to make the right decisions.

"Study the Carotid artery map which is shown here." Captain Neutro was pointing to the wall behind him. "You also have a copy of this in your nucleus." Then Captain Neutro put the WBCs into pairs and each pair selected a different lookout position along the route.

"Okay, Bands, are you ready?" said Phyllis.

"Yes, Sir!" Bands joked and they charged ahead into the darkness.

CHAPTER

6

A bolt of lightning flashed in the tunnel as Bands, Phyllis and the rest of the team, swam to their lookout position. They travelled further up and along the curved tunnel of the Aorta artery. Bands pulled down his cellophane visor screen so he could follow the coordinates of their destination. You had to speed along in the artery tunnel, due to the force created by the heart, and Bands was worried they would miss their exit point.

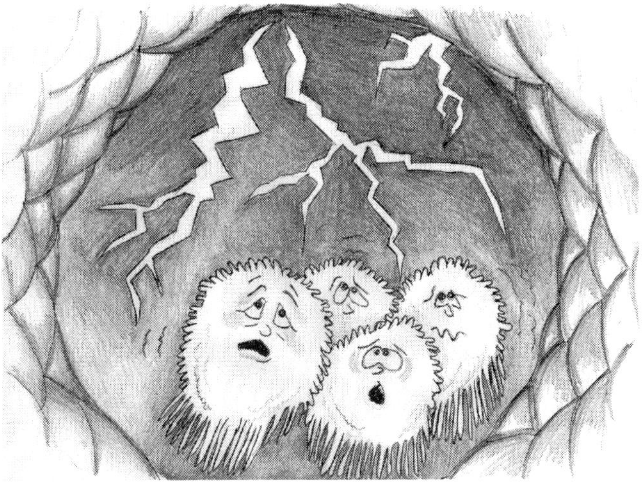

As they reached the top of the tunnel, Bands could see the turning. Then it went dark again and Bands was very glad he could see the exit flashing up on the screen.

"Turn up ahead," shouted Bands. "Hold on!" The pair pushed their bodies to the right to fight the force of the current.

"We travel along this Carotid artery until it splits again," said Phyllis. "We need to take the external artery, the one on the outside."

"Got it! Exit up ahead."

Bands guided the pair of them into the external artery and they both slowed their bodies down so they could find their stakeout position. The red blood cells continued to swim past them at fast speeds, surfing the waves of the current.

Bolts of lightning lit up the area as they continued up the artery. Phyllis led the way and Bands studied his screen looking for a good place to stop.

"Watch out!" Phyllis whispered, as she

dragged herself and Bands over to the tissue wall and crouched down.

"What's the matter?" Bands started to say before Phyllis pulled him to the floor and put one of her legs over his mouth.

"Ssh! They'll hear you!" said Phyllis.

When Bands was quiet, Phyllis put her leg down so he could talk. "Who will hear?" whispered Bands.

"The enemy. I saw two of them up ahead."

"Are you sure? They are supposed to be further along, near the throat?"

"I know what I saw," said Phyllis. "They are just up in front of us. We will need to get closer but I don't think we will be able to get to the lookout position without them spotting us."

"Okay. We need stealth mode now.

Let's use the red blood cells as our shields, and get in close so we can use the micro cell phones to pick up anything they are saying. You ready?"

"Yes, Sir," she whispered back.

Slowly they swam back out into the blood tunnel again, with their heads close to the flow of the plasma, hidden by a large group of bobbing red blood cells. Phyllis tugged on Bands shoulder and pointed out the invader up ahead. Like a silent submarine they made their way to their target.

The two round purple balls were travelling quite slowly, as though they were looking for something or someone. They began to speak.

"This is going to be too easy. Maybe we should stop for a rest," said the more menacing of the two purple bodies.

"But we need to get to the throat. We have our orders," said the younger virus.

"Oh, don't worry about that. I have already spoken to the rest of the team and they are handling the situation at the throat."

"What do you mean?"

"You know! Using our mind powers to trick the cells," laughed the evil virus.

* * *

Bands and Phyllis were close enough they could hear the conversation. "I don't think the other one understands," said Phyllis. "That could be a good thing."

"I wouldn't be too certain of that. Keep listening!" replied Bands.

* * *

The evil-looking flu virus spoke again. "Seriously? Do you not listen?"

The young virus shook his head.

"We have great powers, young one," the older virus continued. "We can trick other cells with our minds. Make them do things we want them to do. Shall I go on?"

The young virus nodded.

"We need to get past the guard cells at the base of the throat. There are machines inside that can make more of us. We use our power to trick them. We fool them into thinking we are like them. They welcome us in through their nucleus, and once inside, we burst open our bodies to release our secret code. This code is put into the machines and, hey presto, it is now making more copies of us!"

"Then what happens, B5," said the eager young virus.

"We make our way out of the nucleus and into the blood stream along with all the other cells. Except now there are millions more of us."

"Wow! That is cool. This is going to be so easy," laughed the young virus.

“Well, we have to strike at the right time,” said B5.

“What do you mean?”

“If we start fighting too soon, there might not be enough copies of us to win. If we start fighting too late, then those annoying white blood cells will have the chance to attack us,” explained B5. “Wait! I’ve just received a message. We are wanted as back up. Full steam ahead to the throat!”

And with that they raced off down the tunnel.

Bands and Phyllis looked at each other. This was not good news.

CHAPTER

7

A large crowd of WBCs were gathered together at the top of the Aorta. Commander Lympho, Captain Neutro and Captain Mono stood at the front, looking serious. Bands and Phyllis drifted into position at the back of the crowd.

"The situation is worse than we thought," shouted Captain Mono. "The flu virus is now beginning to invade the upper part of the body. Open up your screens please?"

The cells did as they were told. On the screen was a map of the body's network system. The arteries and veins were colour coded to show the different paths in the bloodstream.

Captain Neutro spoke. "We know the flu virus began at the base of the throat. The enemy has been able to access the guard cell's nucleus and there are now many more of the viruses. They have been making their way from the throat, down the Aorta, where they are spreading to the shoulders and arms."

"We have positioned teams at the important areas; Carotid artery, Heart and Aorta," said Captain Mono, "but we are concerned at how easily they have been able to multiply in the body."

Bands and Phyllis moved to the front. "We know why, Sir?" said Phyllis. "We managed to hear some of the conversation between two of the viruses. They have the ability to trick or fool cells into thinking they are like them. When they have done this, they are then allowed into their nucleus where they use the copying machine inside. It normally makes more good cells, but now it makes more of them," explained Phyllis.

Bands continued, "When they exit the nucleus, the good cells all think they are like them and therefore don't sound the alarm. The viruses are spreading themselves through the body, slowly and surely, taking their time so they don't get caught. They have been fooling us the whole time!"

Captain Mono and Neutro both looked at Commander Lympho.

"I have seen this before. We need to attack them, but not by sight," said Commander Lympho. "We need to use our special powers to feel their energy. Then we will be able to identify the different cells and which ones are the leaders."

Captain Neutro proceeded to demonstrate how to use this power. He opened up his nucleus and found the settings button. He switched the 'Operation' button from automatic to manual. "Now you will be able to feel their energy, but you must be careful. The override switch does not protect you any more."

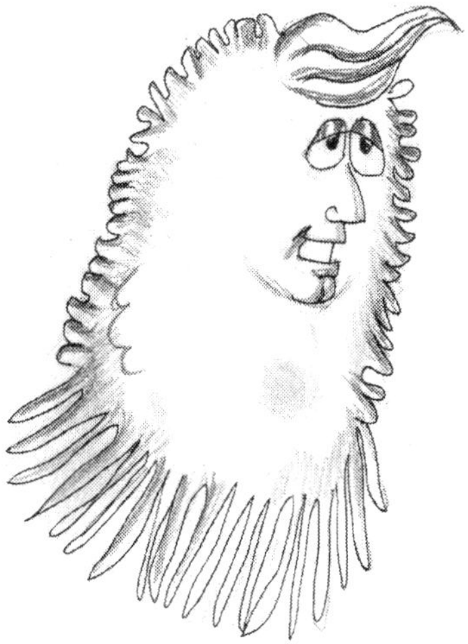

"What does that mean?" asked one of the WBCs.

"We are all linked into the blood network so we know what's going on in the body," said Captain Mono. "We hear the emergency calls, we can plot your coordinates and can communicate with each of you using the cell phones. Switching to manual means you can use your senses more, to feel who and where the enemy is, but you are no longer part of the network. Now you are on your own!"

Bands and Phyllis looked at each other and, without hesitating, switched their buttons to manual. This was their job. Risking their lives to save others is what they were born to do.

"Sir! Where would you like us to start?" they said to Captain Neutro.

"We need you to go to the root of the problem; the guard cells. Now you know how they trick us, you should be able to work out who the enemy is. Attacking them first, will stop them multiplying further into our system. You will need a team to go with you. Do we have any volunteers?"

A handful of WBCs came to the front. Bands thanked them.

"Bands, I would like you to run this operation," said Captain Mono. "Your cell phones will not work so you must make sure you communicate with each other, especially as you are going under cover."

"Watch out for each other and when you think you have succeeded in finding all the dangerous viruses, go to the branch in the Aorta. We will meet you there," said Captain Neutro.

"Where are you going, Sir?" asked Bands.

"We will begin our fight at the Aorta and work our way around the body. Hopefully, we will be able to locate and kill all the viruses, before they get too far in. Once that is under control, I will come and help you. I have faith in you, Bands. I know you can do this."

Bands flushed with pride and he suddenly felt very grown up. He was now being trusted to lead a team and complete a very important task.

"Good luck, soldiers. Until we meet again." And with that Captain Neutro and Captain Mono sped off.

Phyllis looked at Bands. "This is it! You ready?"

"As ready as I'll ever be. This is our job. Let's do it!"

The team knew this would be difficult. For the first time, since they were born in the bone marrow, they were completely on their own.

CHAPTER

8

Bands, Phyllis and the rest of the team swam, as fast they could, up the Aorta to the exit point. Lightning bolts flashed overhead.

Groups of red blood cells glided along the smooth, pink paneled walls, talking and laughing as they went. Bands thought about Haemo and Globin, from earlier that day. '*If only they knew what was happening*,' thought Bands. '*Maybe they wouldn't be so laid back and happy*.'

Bands recognised the exit point up ahead. "Sharp, right turn!" he shouted. The team turned in unison, like a bob sleigh team racing around a corner. From here, they slowed their speed down as they found their way to the Carotid artery.

As the artery split into two paths, Bands could see some WBCs already in action fighting the virus. They were stretching out their bodies and attacking the virus with their suction guns. The virus couldn't fight back, so it was easy to clear away a big group of them.

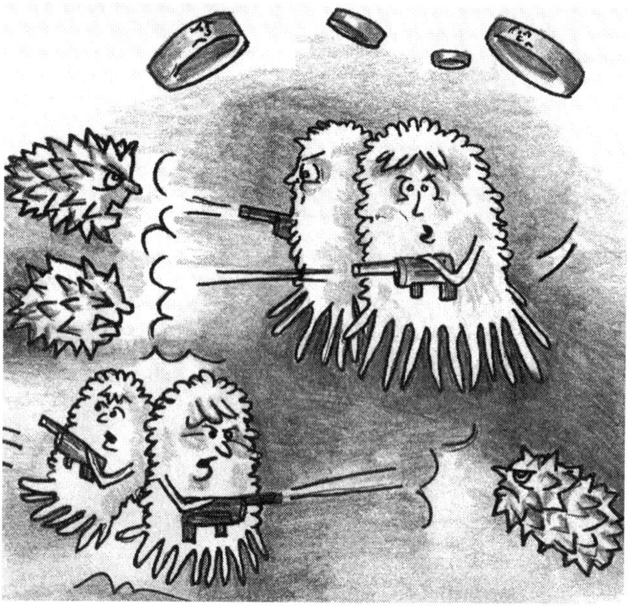

The problem was that there were so many of them. And they kept coming. Bands could see four, five and then six new viruses, each second they were fighting. This wasn't good!

"Okay, team! Keep going! We are nearly at the top," encouraged Bands.

"Sir?" said Phyllis. " Do you think we will be able to stop them?"

Bands knew she had been thinking the same thing as him when they saw the WBCs attacking the viruses. “Of course we will. Remember what Commander Lympho said. We are an army of cells, a creator of life and a phenomenal force. It’s not going to be easy, but it’s our job, Phyllis, and we will do what we have to do.”

“Yes, Sir!” Phyllis cried and the team increased their speed. Up the Carotid artery, one behind the other, single file into the capillaries and through to the surface of the throat.

Once there, Bands led them to a safe place. “Team! We need to spread out and use our cellescopic binoculars. They will light up the search area and alert us to any unusual activity happening here at the throat. If you identify a threat, you must let me know. We can’t radio this in as we have no communication with the base, but we must stay in touch. Is that understood?”

“Yes, Sir!” they all whispered and then, one by one, broke away in formation.

Bands floated over the surface of the throat, keeping to the sides so he would not be seen. He could see the guard cells patrolling the area. They swam up and down and all seemed calm. He moved further up.

Once again, he floated over the surface and, once again, all seemed calm. The guard cells were marching methodically across the area. Bands was just about to leave when he felt a slight shudder across his body. He thought about what Commander Lympho said. ‘*You have to feel the enemy to know who and where they are.*’ He looked again.

At the end of the line of the guard cells,

one of them was not moving and it looked like he was in a trance. He didn't seem to be aware of what was going on around him. Bands approached him.

"Guard!" Bands shouted. The guard stayed quite still. "Guard!" he shouted again. Nothing. Bands stood right in front of him now and looked into his eyes. They were like shiny mirrors, Bands' reflection staring back at him. The guard showed no reaction to Bands standing in front of him at all.

'*This is strange*,' Bands thought to

himself. '*What is going on*?' Bands moved quietly and stood behind the guard. He closed his eyes and concentrated on trying to sense what was around him.

Then he felt it. A warmth, an energy, coming from the front of the guard. Bands opened his eyes. It was just as he thought. He could see him clearly now. The purple virus was positioned in front of the guard cell, moving his body before his eyes. The guard kept staring, not moving a muscle.

"*He's hypnotising him*!" guessed Bands. '*That's how they are getting in.*' He continued to watch. After a couple of minutes, the guard cell opened up his nucleus and the purple enemy swam in. Once the virus had entered, the guard cell woke up oblivious as to what had just happened.

Bands moved further down the lining of the throat. It was just as he feared. There were many more viruses all doing the same thing to other guard cells. Just then Bands noticed Phyllis hovering further down. "Phyllis!" he shouted. Over here!"

Phyllis raced over to Bands. "Sir! I have seen how the virus is getting in. They are being hypnotised into letting them into their nucleus."

"I know, Phyllis. I felt it first and then I saw them. Get a message to the rest of the team. The orders are to shoot on sight. Once the viruses are identified, they need to attack quickly before they get inside the cells. We must shoot every virus we see doing the hypnotizing, or the numbers of the virus getting into the bloodstream will be too many for us to fight."

"Yes, Sir! Reporting now!" Phyllis raced to the rest of the team, while Bands began his search for the other flu viruses. Before it was too late.

CHAPTER

9

Bands pulled down his cellophane visor screen and continued along the throat lining. The screen lit up like it usually did. But now he had to feel the energy coming from the virus. Bands focused all his effort on using his senses and removed his visor screen. He needed to feel if the flu virus was in range and locked down in his firing line. In the darkness, Bands closed his eyes and felt the force of the energy, coming from the virus, guiding him.

Quickly he moved around to find the enemies. It was so weird. Although he couldn't see the virus, he could feel where it was. There was a warmth that radiated out of the virus and flowed around Bands' body. When he felt this heat he knew he was close, and had to concentrate on where the heat was coming from.

As he followed the heat, he could hear the virus talking. 'Let me in, let me in.' It kept repeating it over and over. It was powerful and Bands had to stop listening before he was hypnotised too. Now he knew where the enemy was and could aim. Bands shot the virus with his poisoned gun. He heard it shrivel up and disintegrate, and then he moved onto finding the next virus.

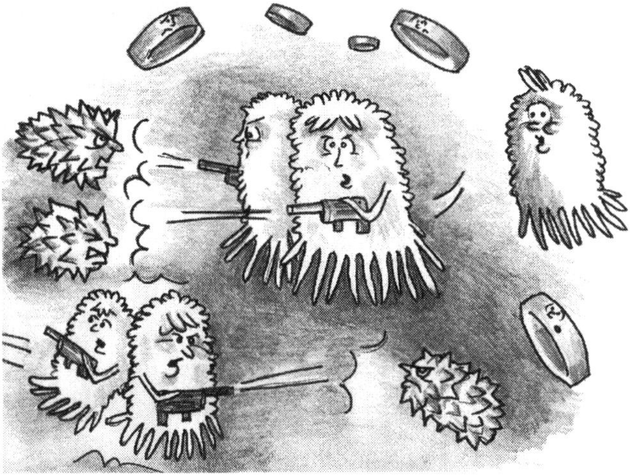

When the viruses realised they were under threat, they tried to move to a different location, but Phyllis and the rest of the team were waiting for them. One by one, they shot the enemies. But each time one virus was killed, Bands saw another up ahead. There were so many of them still here and this was worrying. The viruses, knowing they could be exterminated, began trying to push their way into the cells. Bands and his team had to be careful to shoot the virus and not the guard cell.

"Hold still!" Bands ordered the guard cell, as he aimed at the next virus attempting a break in. He shot. The virus sank down dead at the guard cell's feet.

The fighting continued for one long hour and then darkness fell. Finally, there were no more viruses in the area.

"Great job everyone," praised Bands, as they all grouped at the exit by the Carotid artery. "We have completed our mission and although it was successful, our job is not over. Now we need to join the battle and help our fellow soldiers. To the Aorta!"

The team swam away in single file. Phyllis was directly behind Bands.

"Sir! Do you think we are winning the fight at the Aorta?"

"Captain Neutro said he would come and join us when they had the situation under control." Bands turned to look at Phyllis. "So do you think we are winning the fight?"

Phyllis was silent. She understood. Bands faced the front and increased his speed through the tunnel. There was no time to lose.

Turning left, then right, the team in unison, made their way along the Carotid artery. Cracks and crackles echoed in the tunnel and lightning bolts lit up the narrow pathway.

Red blood cells hurried past them in the opposite direction. '*Off on their job to take oxygen around the body*,' Bands thought. '*No worries about fighting for them.*' Bands actually felt jealous of the red blood cells. But just for a minute.

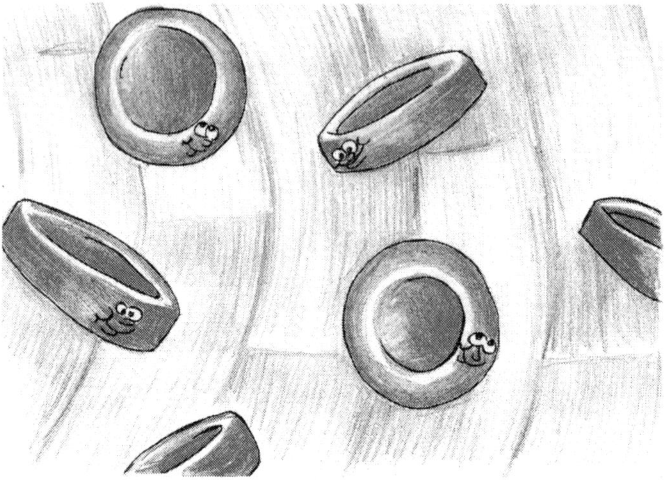

'*Snap out of it,*' Bands said to himself. '*You are a white blood cell. This is your job. The job you were born to do.*'

"Did you say something?" asked Phyllis.

"Er, no, sorry. Just mumbling to myself. Ignore me!" Bands could see the exit point. "Destination up ahead," he shouted back to his team. As they sailed into the branch of the top of the Aorta, they slowed down and looked around for the other white blood cells. Bands was desperate to see Captain Neutro and Mono.

They waited in silence, knowing that each minute meant it was worse than they thought. No one showed. How long should they keep on waiting? No one knew. This had never happened before.

Phyllis looked at Bands. "Sir, what should we do now?"

Bands stared at the faces of the white blood cells, all looking at him quizzingly. He was in charge. He had to lead. He had to decide.

"Open up your nucleus, please?" Bands said. "Go to settings and switch the button from manual to automatic." All the cells did as they were told. "You are now back online. Your mission is to find and destroy all the flu viruses already copied and in the blood system. If you find yourself in trouble, radio for back up. Good luck team."

The WBCs shot off into the artery path. Bands stayed still. He looked down at his nucleus screen. The settings button was still turned to manual. Bands knew he had to carry on finding these dangerous viruses, the ones doing the hypnotising. '*There has to be more of them in the body*," Bands thought to himself. '*And where was Captain Neutro and his team? They must be in trouble. But am I able to do this on my own? I have to try.*'

He closed his screen and propelled himself down the tunnel and into the war!

CHAPTER

10

Red blood cells rushed past Bands on their way through the padded artery. He came to a part of the Aorta where it branched off into the shoulders. Bands could see lots of red blood cells, all bunched together like humans in inflatable rings at the start of a water slide. What was happening? Why weren't they moving along as normal?

Just then, Bands saw Haemo and Globin ahead of him. "Hey, Globin! What's going on?"

Globin turned around at the sound of his name. "Hey! Look, Haemo! It's the little dude from earlier."

Bands pushed past the other red blood cells in his way. "Why all the traffic?"

"Oh, that!" said Haemo. "Some ugly bugs are causing trouble. Your mates are doing their best to get rid of them, but there are so many, man!"

"You joining the fight or do you wanna come with us? Once we get through that is," said Globin.

"Thanks guys but my job is to attack those ugly bugs. Maybe I'll catch up with you later?"

"Yeh, that would be cool, man!" answered Haemo and Globin together. "Catch you later."

Bands waved to Haemo and Globin and then squeezed his way through the other red blood cells blocking his path. The tunnel curved to the right and then went upwards. Bands raced as fast as he could and went over the top.

What a sight he saw! Hundreds and hundreds of purple, spiky viruses spread out all over the area like toast covered with blackberry jam.

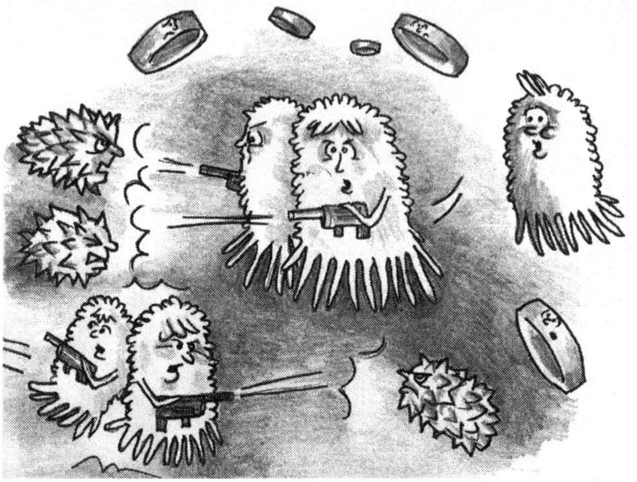

Teams of WBCs were stretching out their bodies and ingesting the deadly enemy, but it wasn't making much of a difference. The viruses continued to grow in number. While one WBC was busy, chasing and shooting a virus, another virus managed to escape and carry on his path to the arms. They were spreading fast.

Taking out his gun, Bands started to shoot at the spiky enemy. One, then two, and then, three. Still more came. But these were ordinary viruses, not the special hypnotising ones. He needed to find them quickly and stop them from making more copies. He couldn't hear what was happening with the rest of his team, as he was still in manual operation. He had to rely on his senses. Bands closed his eyes and concentrated. Suddenly someone bumped into him.

"Bands! I've been calling you over the cell phone. Why didn't you answer?"

Bands opened his eyes to see Captain Neutro standing in front of him.

"Sir! I apologise. Still in manual mode," answered Bands, delighted to see Captain Neutro again.

"I see. Well, the rest of your team radioed in and Phyllis has given me an update. Looks like you did a good job."

"Sir! I don't understand. If we did such a good job, why are there so many of the viruses still here?" Bands asked.

Neutro sighed. "We can't work it out. Stopping the viruses at the source of the problem in the throat should have helped the situation. Commander Lympho has called for back up. The Antibodies are on their way. We just have to pray that it's enough."

Just then they heard a low buzz overhead. Bands looked up and saw a group of molecules, like small helicopters, hovering above. The antibodies! They were always called in by Commander Lympho to help in any battles where the WBCs were outnumbered. The antibodies flew over the area, spraying the viruses with a special paralysing poison. This slowed the viruses down and allowed the WBCs to suck up many more of them in one go. Captain Neutro and

Bands swam back into the line of fire to continue the fight.

As Bands carried on shooting at the viruses, he couldn't help wondering why the situation was not under control. Hadn't they killed all the viruses in the Carotid artery? Bands thought back to the operation he went on with Phyllis. He remembered the two purple viruses talking about how they tricked the guard cell into letting them in. What else did they say? Something about they will think we are like them.

"*That's it!* " said Bands to himself, suddenly realising. "*That's how they are doing it!*" He needed to tell Captain Neutro and fast.

CHAPTER

11

The purple virus, B5, was staring at a WBC standing at the entrance to a tunnel. “Let me in! Let me in!” he whispered. Waving his body in front of the cell, made the cell go dizzy and put it into a trance-like state.

"This is so easy," B5 said out loud, as he entered the cell's nucleus. The cell began to jiggle around until his middle burst open. Lots of new purple virus copies rushed out and began to make their way into the blood system. Then B5 came out.

"Those white blood cells have no idea I'm turning these cells into viruses. They think the cells look like they normally do," B5 laughed. "They can't see they are now disguised. Ha, ha!"

The virus waited until all the copies had exited the dead cell's body and fled up the artery, onto the next unsuspecting cell.

* * *

Neutro and Bands put away their cellescopic binoculars. They were hiding in one of the cushioned folds of the tunnel and had seen the whole thing.

"You were right, Bands! Good work. They must have been using this cunning plan for ages. That's why there are so many of them. They look like ordinary cells not viruses. I need to radio this in."

After Neutro phoned the base, Bands said, "Sir! Would you trust me to help find and destroy the viruses like this B5?"

"Of course, Bands, but you will need support and you must go back online. We need to know where you are."

Bands looked at Captain Neutro. “I can’t do that, Sir! I see the viruses doing the hypnotising if I use my power. I can only do that in manual.”

Captain Neutro looked back at Bands. “Okay, I understand. It’s risky, but it’s your call. Only this time, I’m coming with you. Let’s go.”

The two WBCs swam around the curved tunnel of the subclavian artery in the shoulder. They went past hundreds of WBCs and Antibodies still fighting the virus. Bands didn't see any of this. He had his eyes closed, focused only on finding the invisible invaders.

"Sir! Up ahead. I feel one," Bands said. Bands and Neutro slowed down, moving cautiously. They couldn't let the virus know they were on to him. The virus was working his powers on another cell, while Bands pretended to swim past them. As soon as the virus was behind him, Bands turned and locked the virus in his firing line. He shot his gun and the virus fell to the floor in a heap.

"Well done, Bands," praised Neutro. "Time to find some others."

The next area they arrived at had at least four or five B5s hypnotising the other cells.

“You take the left side, Bands and I’ll go round the right. That way we shouldn’t miss any.”

Neutro glided around to the right, as Bands closed his eyes and waited. He felt the heat first. Then a glow appeared in his mind, the outline of the virus glistening with infra red light. Focusing on the light, Bands could aim and fire. He shot one, then another, then another. That made three now.

Moving around to the left, Bands saw another glowing light. He took aim and was about to fire, when he saw who the virus was staring at. It was Captain Neutro!

“Let me in, let me in! “ the B5 repeated over and over. Neutro’s eyes were starting to glaze over. He was going into a trance. It was too late. Neutro was already under the spell of the virus.

Bands needed to shoot the virus quickly, but he had to be careful. If he fired now, he might kill Captain Neutro? Bands fingers were shaking as he held out his gun. He tried to move himself into a position so he had a clear view of the virus. But the virus was too close to Neutro and any second he would be close enough to enter into Neutro's body.

Bands had no choice. He had to shoot. He squeezed the trigger and fired. Bands opened his eyes to see Captain Neutro crumpled on the floor in a heap.

"Captain Neutro! Are you alright?" asked Bands, rushing to his side. Neutro's eyes remained closed. Oh no! What had he done? He'd killed his hero and his friend. He'd made a mess of everything. Bands slumped down on the floor next to Neutro's body.

"What happened, Bands? One minute I

was tracking a virus, and the next, I'm sitting here with you in what looks like an explosion of blackcurrant jam," said Neutro, shaking his head from side to side.

"Thank goodness, you're alright. I thought I'd killed you." Bands explained the whole story.

Neutro looked at Bands. "It seems I owe you my life, but we don't have time to talk now. We must carry on."

"Yes, Sir!" said Bands and they charged off together to complete their mission.

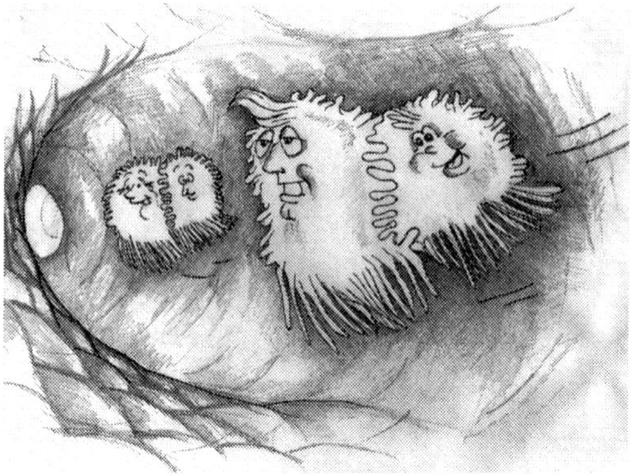

CHAPTER

12

Bands' team was spread out along the artery tunnel, each one firing at the enemy in a controlled way. This was down to Phyllis. She knew how to organise them and he was very proud of her.

"Glad to have you back online, Sir!" Phyllis said smiling.

"Glad to be back." Bands returned the smile. "Are our orders still the same?"

"Yes, Sir, although we can now say that the threat to our human is greatly reduced. It seems you found all the main enemy leaders so now we are managing to chase and consume the virus copies. Well done, Sir!"

“Okay, then let’s finish this job.”

Phyllis, Bands and the rest of the team continued to shoot the remaining viruses. Overhead, the Antibodies could be heard flying away, a sure sign that the worst was over. Thunder and lightning crashed in the distance, lighting up the WBCs chasing the virus like cats chasing mice.

Hours turned into days and eventually they heard the loud signal they had been waiting for. The suppressor cells shouted out the good news. “Stop the fighting! Stop the fighting! The virus has been destroyed.”

Bands and Phyllis hugged each other. “We did it!” said Phyllis.

“I couldn’t have done it without you,” said Bands. “Teamwork!”

“Okay, guys,” said Captain Neutro, speaking to the whole team now gathered next to Bands. “Great job! Now, go and rest and that’s an order!”

“Yes, Sir!” replied the team in unison.

* * *

Later on, the WBCs were once again summoned to the Great Hall of the Vena Cava. Commander Lympho spoke to the crowd about the mission and how he had been made aware of some very special acts of bravery that had to be recognised.

"One cell, in particular, showed tremendous courage," said Commander Lympho, "demonstrating that sometimes we have to put others before ourselves, and make difficult decisions if we are to survive. That cell is Bands. Would you like to step up to the front please?"

The cells all cheered as Bands stood next to Commander Lympho. A large group of red blood cells rushed past, surfing the wave, and joined in with the cheering.

"Hey, Bands! Well done, little dude!" shouted Haemo.

"Yeh, nice one," added Globin.

"Thanks, guys," shouted Bands. "Maybe we can catch up later. There's still lots I want to ask you."

"You and your questions," laughed Haemo. "Sorry, little dude. We have to go."

Bands floated towards Haemo and Globin. "Where you going? I'll meet you?"

Haemo and Globin looked at each other.

"Sorry, little guy. You can't come with us this time."

"We're moving on, man. Our time is up," said Globin.

"You mean…" was all Bands could manage to say.

"Hey, don't sweat it. We knew it would happen soon. And at least it's been a ride!"

"It sure has," said Haemo. "The best ride ever, man!"

"Take care, little dude. Was great to meet you," they both said, before shooting off down the dark tunnel.

Bands turned to face the crowd of WBCs, knowing he would never see Haemo or Globin again. Master Baso appeared by his side.

"Bands. You knew this would happen. It is a fact of life, all blood cells die one day."

"I know. I just didn't expect it this quickly."

"Their life spans may be short, but they know how to live life to the full. Remember that. You must go on. Your job goes on and so does your life. In this battle you showed great bravery, and you need to continue to be brave now with your team. Can you do that?"

"Yes, Sir!' replied Bands.

"I know it's hard, but it does get easier. Now, go and 'cellebrate' with your team. They need you."

Bands knew Master Baso was right. He was always right. The WBCs needed him. They were a team and soon there would be another battle. Of that he was certain.

GLOSSARY - USEFUL WORDS

adrenaline – a hormone produced by the body during stress or exciting situations

antibody – a special protein that helps destroy or neutralise enemies

artery – a vessel that carries blood with oxygen away from the heart

bacteria – a tiny creature with one cell. Some bacteria cause infections.

band cell – a very young WBC that has recently been made in the bone marrow

blood – contains white and red cells and platelets floating in a liquid called plasma

bloodstream – the body's transport system

bone marrow – a thick spongy tissue in the middle of bones

capillary – a tiny blood vessel between the artery and vein

carbon dioxide – a gas we breathe out

cell – a very small living thing. All living things are made up of cells.

energy – the power that makes things work

force – a push or a pull

germs – small living things that can cause disease

heart – a hard working muscle

lungs –large organs in charge of your breathing

microbes – another name for germs

molecules – tiny pieces made up of atoms (that everything is made of)

nucleus – the central, most important part of a cell

organ - part of the body (heart, kidneys, liver, lungs)

oxygen – a gas we breathe in

plasma – a yellowish liquid

platelets – blood cells which help blood to clot

red blood cells – blood cells that carry oxygen

tissue – a group of cells that stick together

vein – vessel that carries blood without oxygen back to the heart

virus – a small infectious molecule that multiplies inside living things

white blood cells – neutrophil, basophil, lymphocyte and **monocyte** – fight infection in the body

28672412R00072

Printed in Great Britain
by Amazon